GETTING TO KNOW
MEXICO

Carmen Irizarry

PASSPORT BOOKS
a division of *NTC Publishing Group*
Lincolnwood, Illinois USA

Editor: Lynne Williams
Design: Edward Kinsey
Illustrations: Hayward Art Group
Consultant: Keith Lye

Photographs: Tony and Marion Morrison,
ZEFA, Tony Hutchings, Mexicolore, Bridgeman
Art Library, BBC Hulton Picture Library,
NASA, Mexican Embassy

Front cover: Tony and Marion Morrison, ZEFA
Back cover: Tony and Marion Morrison

This edition first published in 1991 by Passport Books,
a division of NTC Publishing Group,
4255 West Touhy Avenue, Lincolnwood (Chicago), Illinois 60646-1975 U.S.A.
Copyright © 1991, 1987 Franklin Watts Limited.
Library of Congress Catalog Card Number: 90-61388

Contents

Introduction	5
The land	6
The people	8
Where people live	10
Mexico City	12
Fact file: land and population	14
Home life	16
Shops and shopping	18
Cooking and eating	20
Pastimes and sports	22
News and broadcasting	24
Fact file: home life and leisure	26
Farming and fishing	28
Natural resources	30
Industry and trade	32
Transportation	34
Fact file: economy and trade	36
Education	38
The arts	40
The making of modern Mexico	42
Mexico in the modern world	44
Fact file: government and world role	46
Index	48

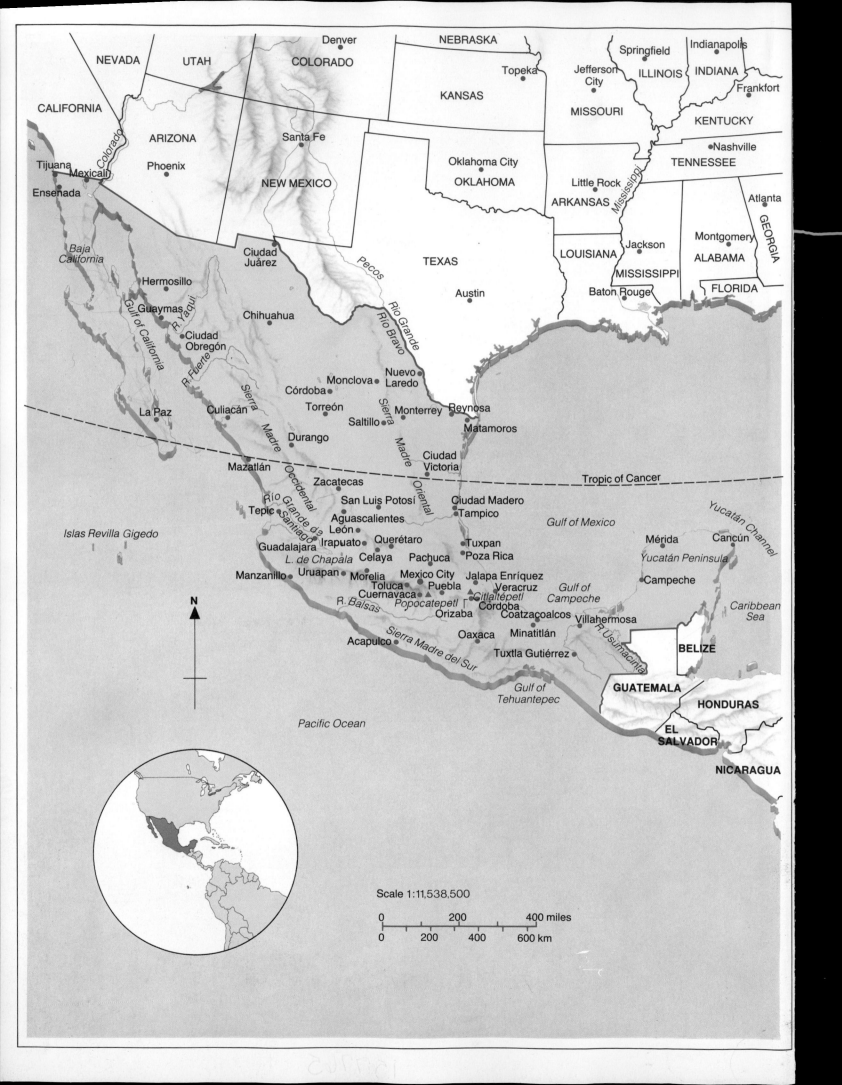

Introduction

Mexico occupies a unique position between the continents of America. It forms the southernmost part of North America, and has strong historical and economic links with the United States. The people and culture of Mexico, however, have greater ties with the countries of Latin America. Thus the country bridges two vast and very different civilizations.

Mexico is a fascinating blend of Indian and Spanish cultures. This mixture is reflected in Mexican life-styles, customs and beliefs and ancient traditions. Mexico is, however, changing fast. Its people are eager for economic and social progress. The country is now a place of great contrasts, where new industry and high technology are eclipsing many of the old ways.

In just a few decades, Mexico has been transformed from a relatively poor country to a far more prosperous and industrialized nation ready to play a prominent role in the affairs of the world.

Above: Remains of ancient Indian civilizations are found in many parts of Mexico. This is a Mayan Temple at Palenque.

Below: A main road into Mexico City. Expressways and high-rise buildings are very typical of the new Mexico.

The land

Mexico is a long, narrow country bordered by the Pacific Ocean to the west, and the Gulf of Mexico and the Caribbean Sea to the east. Extending down the west coast is a long peninsula known as Baja California. In the southern region another great landmass – the Yucatán Peninsula – thrusts far into the Gulf of Mexico.

The country's landscape is extremely varied. It includes deserts, grasslands, snow-capped mountains and humid tropical forests. In the north, where the land is arid or semi-arid, temperatures can range from very hot to bitter cold. The southern coastlands, in contrast, have a sub-tropical or tropical climate and lush vegetation. In the south, too, there is a rainy season, between May and October.

The Pacific coastal plains are very arid in the north and give way to tropical, humid conditions in the south. The Yucatán and the Gulf Coast form the largest lowland area in Mexico. Its northern parts are dry while others are covered by swamps and lagoons.

Above: Pine forests cover the slopes of the Sierra Madre Occidental mountain range, near Toluca, in central Mexico.

Left: Oaxaca in southern Mexico lies at an altitude of 1,500 m (4,921 ft) above sea level. It is not easy for farmers to grow crops in this arid land.

Left: Acapulco, on the Pacific coast, has a humid tropical climate.

Below: Tropical plants, such as bananas, grow in profusion along river valleys, as here in Jalisco State.

Altitude, however, is the dominant physical feature in Mexico. Beginning south of Mexico City, and running north like the arms of a letter Y, are two great mountain chains – the Sierra Madre Occidental and the Sierra Madre Oriental. Among their peaks are Orizaba (Citlatépetl), the country's highest point, and the famous Popacatépetl, whose Indian name means "Smoking Mountain". Both are dormant volcanoes over 5,000 m (16,500 ft) high. The Southern Highlands, or Sierra Madre del Sur, extend from Mexico City along the Pacific coast.

The largest and most important feature of Mexico is, however, the Central Plateau which extends from the United States border to south of Mexico City. It rises to altitudes between 1,000 and 2,000 m (3,300 and 6,600 ft). The Plateau covers over half of Mexico and contains most of the major cities. Its fertile land and equable climate are able provide much of Mexico's food requirements.

The people

Modern Mexico is the product of two very different civilizations – the American Indian and the Spanish. These two cultures have blended to form a unique Mexican way of life.

The first settlers in what is now Mexico were Indian peoples who crossed into North America from Asia several thousand years BC. In time they formed into many distinct tribes and built great civilizations. The Mayas left exquisite sculptures, temples and made many scientific discoveries. Other Indian empires also flourished, including the Toltec, Zapotec and Mixtec.

When the Spanish first arrived in Mexico in 1519, the most powerful tribe were the Aztecs. They were quickly defeated by the Spanish and from 1522 to 1821, Mexico was a colony of Spain and called *New Spain*. Over the centuries the Spaniards and Indian peoples intermarried. Today nearly 80 per cent of the Mexican population are of mixed ancestry or *Mestizos*.

Above: Girls about to take their First Communion. The Catholic faith plays a very important part in Mexican life.

Below: Any crowd of people will illustrate the mixture of Indian and Spanish races that form the Mexican population.

Above: A street trader selling fruit pieces.

Below: Businessmen in Mexico City.

Above: A seller of models made from spare parts.

Below: A stone mason. His forebears carved temples.

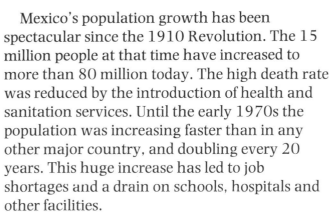

Mexico's population growth has been spectacular since the 1910 Revolution. The 15 million people at that time have increased to more than 80 million today. The high death rate was reduced by the introduction of health and sanitation services. Until the early 1970s the population was increasing faster than in any other major country, and doubling every 20 years. This huge increase has led to job shortages and a drain on schools, hospitals and other facilities.

Above: Children with their paintings.

Below: The bass player of a *mariachi* group.

Although Mexican culture is a mixture of the Spanish and Indian civilizations, the people themselves are largely Indian in origin. Over 50 Indian dialects are still spoken. Spanish is, however, the official language and the majority of people speak it. Many people speak both Spanish and at least one Indian dialect.

The majority of Mexicans are Roman Catholics as a result of the Spanish influence. The great Christian festivals are celebrated with much pageantry and ritual by a large part of the population.

Where people live

The most densely populated parts of Mexico are on the southern plains of the fertile Central Plateau. The most sparsely inhabited regions are the country's two peninsulas – Baja California to the north and the Yucatán in the southeast.

Since the 1950s there has been a large scale migration from the rural areas to the towns and cities. The prospects of a better job and better living conditions are the main reasons for this drift. Generally improved transportation and communications have also made migration easier. By the 1980s only 20 per cent of the population still lived in villages with 2,500 or less people.

Today, nearly 30 per cent of the population live in the country's three largest cities, Mexico City, Guadalajara and Monterrey. Mexico City, however, has seven times the population of Guadalajara.

Above: A remote Indian village in southern Mexico. Many people have left such places to seek work in the cities.

Left: Taxco, southwest of Mexico City, was founded as a silver-mining town by the Spanish in the 16th century.

The spectacular growth of the cities has caused many problems. As the numbers grew, housing and municipal services began to break down. Like many other urban areas in the developing world, Mexico City is now ringed by low-grade housing where newcomers live while they look for work.

More than 30 million Mexicans, the single largest group of the population, make their homes in medium to large-sized towns and provincial capitals. The colonial architecture of these towns, with their elegant *plazas* is often outstanding – stylish, solid and usually well-built.

Such towns have also grown in recent years and many new buildings have been constructed. But their inhabitants are fortunate. These towns usually lack the unhealthy conditions, pollution and overcrowding of the large cities. They are mostly well laid out, and their people lead a less hectic way of life. Town dwellers may be poorer than those who work in the large cities, but their lifestyles are generally considered to be more pleasant.

Above: Cities have grown up around Mexico's many sea-ports. This is Acapulco on the Pacific coast.

Below: A modern development which houses prosperous workers from Mexico City.

Mexico City

Mexico City is the capital of Mexico, the world's largest city and most ancient settlement in the Americas. It is built on the site of a drained lake where the Aztecs settled in the 14th century and built their capital, Tenochtitlán.

The city was destroyed in 1521 by the conquering Spaniards, who immediately began reconstruction around a great new square called the Zócalo. The Zócalo is still the heart of the old city. On one side of it is the cathedral, and on another is the National Palace, the seat of Mexican government. This section of the old city, with its grid-like layout, palaces and mansions, is the heart of the modern capital.

Mexico City has many famous landmarks and monuments commemorating Mexico's history. It also has one of the tallest buildings in the Americas, the 44-story Latin-American Tower. The city's main thoroughfare is the eight-lane highway, the Paseo de la Reforma. There is also a subway system, opened in 1969.

Above: Dominating the city is the Latin American tower which is 181 m (595 ft) high.

Below: Some of Mexico City's landmarks. They reflect centuries of Indian and Spanish civilization.

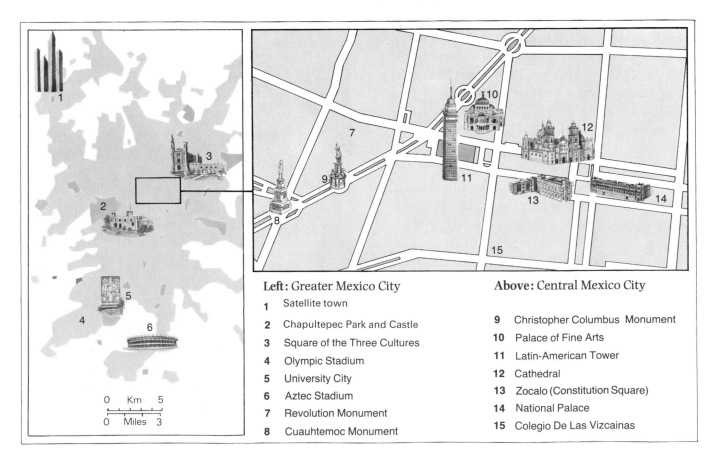

Left: Greater Mexico City

1   Satellite town
2   Chapultepec Park and Castle
3   Square of the Three Cultures
4   Olympic Stadium
5   University City
6   Aztec Stadium
7   Revolution Monument
8   Cuauhtemoc Monument

Above: Central Mexico City

9   Christopher Columbus Monument
10   Palace of Fine Arts
11   Latin-American Tower
12   Cathedral
13   Zocalo (Constitution Square)
14   National Palace
15   Colegio De Las Vizcainas

Mexico City is the country's most important industrial base. Served by efficient road, rail and air links, it has a huge concentration of industries, including oil refining, textiles and clothing manufacture, and food processing. Half of the elcctricity generated in Mexico is used by these industries, which also employ 60 per cent of the city's total workforce. Tourism is also one of the major contributors to the city's economy.

In education and culture, Mexico City is equally important. The world-famous Palace of Fine Arts and the Museum of Anthropology are located here. The city also has nearly a quarter of Mexico's schools, as well as a vast university.

The rapid growth of its population is the city's greatest social problem, for there is much overcrowding. The city also suffers greatly from air pollution. The surrounding mountains unfortunately help to trap the fumes from factories and cars.

Above: Mexico City sprawls over a vast area. In the foreground is the splendid Palace of Fine Arts.

Below: A disastrous earthquake in 1985 brought down many buildings in the city, causing great loss of life.

Fact file: land and population

Key facts

Location: Mexico lies roughly between latitudes 33° and 15° North, and straddles the Tropic of Cancer. It is the third largest country in Latin America, and is bounded by the US to the north and by Guatemala and Belize to the south.

Main parts: Mexico is divided into 31 states, and one federal district, Mexico City, Mexico includes two large peninsulas: Baja California in the northwest (1,220 km/758 miles long); and in the south, the Yucatán Peninsula.

Area: 1,972,547 sq km (761,605 sq miles).

Population: 83,593,000 (1988 estimate).

Capital: Mexico City

Major cities (1986 estimates of metropolitan areas):
Mexico City (18,748,000)
Guadalajara (2,587,000)
Monterrey (2,335,000)
Puebla (1,217,600)
Léon (946,800)
Torréon (729,800)
San Luis Potosí (601,900)
Ciudad Juárez (595,700)
Mérida (580,300)

Other cities (1980 census populations):
Culiacán (560,000)
Mexicali (510,000)
Tijuana (461,000)

Language: Spanish is the official language. Indian languages are also spoken, including Maya, Mixtec, Náhuatl, Otomí and Zapotec.

Highest point: Orizaba (Citlaltépetl). an extinct, snow-capped volcano, southeast of Mexico City, 5,700 m (18,700 ft) above sea-level. It is North America's third highest peak.

Longest river: The Rio Bravo (Rio Grande in the US). The river's total length is 3,925 km (1,880 miles), of which about 2,100 km (1,305 miles) form part of Mexico's northeastern border with the US.

Largest lake: Lake Chapala, in the state of Jalisco, measures 86 km (53 miles) in length by 25 km (16 miles) at its widest.

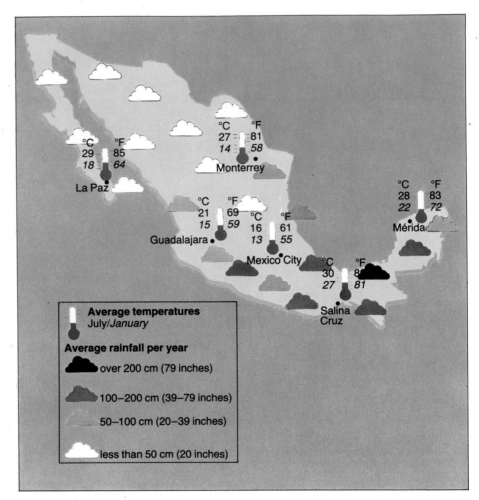

Average temperatures July/*January*

Average rainfall per year
- over 200 cm (79 inches)
- 100–200 cm (39–79 inches)
- 50–100 cm (20–39 inches)
- less than 50 cm (20 inches)

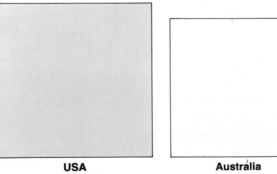

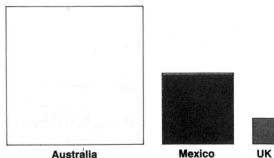

USA Australia Mexico UK

△ **A land area comparison**
Mexico's 1,972,547 sq km (761,605 sq m) of territory make it a small country in comparison with the US, which has 9,370,000 sq km (3,600,000 sq m), or Australia with 7,650,000 sq km (2,470,000 sq m). But Mexico is far larger than many European countries. Britain, for example, has a land area of only 229,979 sq km (88,759 sq m) and is therefore eight times smaller than Mexico.

Cities and towns 71%   Country 29%

△ **Where people live**
Cities and towns account for more than seven-tenths of Mexico's population. Both Baja California and Yucatán are sparsely populated.

Australia 2 per sq km

USA 26 per sq km

Mexico 42 per sq km

UK 242 per sq km

△ **A population density comparison**
Mexico's population has increased greatly in recent years. But world-wide it is still rated as medium-low. There is a very unequal distribution between rural areas and the crowded, ever-expanding cities.

🏢	Major cities
—	Main routeways
⚓	Main ports

Tijuana
Mexicali
Cuidad Juárez
Chihuahua
Guaymas
Culiacán
Monterrey
San Luis Potosí
Tampico
Mérida
Mazatlán
Mexico City
Veracruz
Coatzacoalcos
León
Guadalajara
Puebla
Manzanillo
Lázaro Cárdenas
Acapulco
Salina Cruz
Puerto Madero

▷ **Major population centers**
Most people live on the Central Plateau. The areas in and round the larger ports also have substantial populations.

Home life

The Mexican's home may be a modern urban apartment, a simple village dwelling, or a shanty on the edge of an industrial town. It may even be a mansion situated in an elegant quarter of Mexico City. Whatever its size or style, the house usually shelters a large and close-knit family.

In Mexico the average household has between five and six members. Many households include several generations. The grandparents share in the education of the young as much as the father and mother. The grandparents are left to look after the house and children if both parents go out to work.

Grown-up, unmarried children – especially girls – almost always live at home. Girls continue to share in the running of the household even if they have an outside job. When they marry some may move in with their in-laws. Close contact is the main rule of family life in Mexico.

Above: A traditional house in a small village in central Mexico.

Below: A birthday provides the occasion for a family gathering near Veracruz.

Left: A living room with simple and practical furniture. There is a radio and record player, but no television.

Below: This family, living on the outskirts of Mexico City, is a typical example of the modern urban family.

It is almost always the women – either female members of the family, or a maid if there is one – who do the cooking and cleaning in a Mexican household. Cooking is usually elaborate, because mealtimes are regarded as important family occasions. For this reason the family home, however small, will generally have a proper dining room where old and young can sit down together. Bedrooms are nearly always shared, too, regardless of the social and economic standing of the family.

After the evening meal, the family will usually listen to the radio or gather round the television set. Throughout the year there are special celebrations to enjoy. Frequent national holidays herald parades and fireworks. Weddings and christenings bring gatherings of friends and relations which are followed by large, lavish parties. Mexicans love music and dancing, and spare no expense when a member of the family has reason to celebrate. Old or young, married or single, most Mexicans think, live and enjoy themselves as a family unit.

Shops and shopping

Most visitors to Mexico are immediately impressed by the vivid colours of goods on sale in the shops. Among the brightest are traditional blankets and shawls, hand-painted figurines, shiny red chilies and gleaming copperware.

In villages or rural areas trading often takes place at an outdoor market, or *tiangui*. The *tiangui* consists of a length of canvas on which the goods are laid, with a second piece hoisted above to make a roof. There are no fixed prices at *tianguis*, everyone haggles. The general bustle at outdoor markets is sometimes accompanied by lively music provided by local bands.

Most towns also have indoor markets housed in large, airy halls which were built at the beginning of the century or even earlier. Large numbers of street vendors can be seen in most cities. They sell almost anything from pet animals to toys and chinaware.

Above: In rural areas many people bring their goods to sell in open-air markets.

Below: Large indoor markets are common in every town and city. They sell a vast range of goods.

Small shops and stalls are found throughout Mexico. Handicraft dealers sell local pottery, silverwork and woven baskets, while the local grocery store will have shelves laden with food, especially herbs and spices.

Shopping in Mexico is often a social activity, as in many other countries. While shopping many people catch up on the local news and gossip. Local shops are open long hours and attract many people because of the personal attention given to customers. Supermarkets are also popular, especially with the more affluent families who are able to drive to the stores by car and so take advantage of cheaper bulk purchases.

Shopping in the large cities, such as Mexico City and Guadalajara, is often more impersonal, although the choice of goods is wider. As well as large markets, these cities have elegant boutiques and busy department stores which are open from 9.30 a.m. to 5.30 p.m. Their prices are too high for many people and they cater mostly for the affluent Mexican and the tourist trade.

Above: A local shop. Small grocers are very common and offer a wide range of foods.

Below: A shopping arcade in Guanajuato. It stocks modern merchandise and the latest fashions.

Cooking and eating

For Mexicans, meals are usually family occasions. Breakfast is always simple, consisting of coffee and bread or buns. Until recent times lunch was an elaborate meal. In small towns and in rural areas it is still the most important meal for most families. Dinner has, however, now become the main meal in large cities, where the distance between home and work may be considerable. The family can be together for a meal only in the evening.

Meals are usually accompanied by drinks such as fruit juices. Adults often have wine and beer, and sometimes the strong spirit known as *tequila*.

Mexico has given the world one of the most distinctive styles of cooking, and also a great many foodstuffs. Tomatoes, chocolate, vanilla and peanuts are just a few of the foods that originally came from Mexico and are now eaten throughout the world.

Above: The family have a modern kitchen. Most meals are eaten in a dining room.

Below: A family sits down to an outdoor meal. On the menu are chicken, *tortillas* and soft drinks.

Left: A snack can be obtained quickly at a *tortilla* bar. A wide range of fillings are available.

Below: *Chili con carne* is made with meat, beans, chili peppers, onions and spices. It is one of Mexico's most famous dishes.

Corn is the country's most important basic food. Since ancient times it has been used to make flat pancakes called *tortillas*. They are eaten like bread or made into a snack called a *taco* with different fillings. Beans are another important ingredient in the Mexican diet, either cooked and eaten on their own, or mixed with other ingredients. Beans are used in one of the most famous Mexican dishes – *chili con carne.*

Mexico has many other dishes that are not well known outside the country. One of these is *mole poblano.* It consists of chicken or turkey cooked in an elaborate sauce or *mole* made up of 30 to 40 ingredients including unsweetened chocolate, which gives the dish its brown color. Like many Mexican dishes, it is a blend of Indian and Spanish cooking.

Throughout Mexico *tortilla* and *taco* stands provide people with quick, freshly cooked meals at any time of the day. Most large towns and cities also have restaurants offering a variety of national and international dishes. These are popular and bustling places at lunchtime, when they are filled with workers and shoppers.

Pastimes and sports

Many of Mexico's pastimes and sports have their origins in Spain, but games from other countries, such as soccer, volleyball and tennis, are also popular.

Mexico played host to the world for the 1968 Olympic Games, and has been the venue for soccer's World Cup finals in 1970 and 1986. Soccer is the country's leading spectator sport. Matches held on local grounds or in huge stadiums such as the Azteca Stadium in Mexico City attract large, enthusiastic crowds. Other spectator sports with a large following include bullfighting introduced from Spain and baseball from the US. People also like the handball game known as *jai alai*, which originated in the Basque region of Spain.

Jogging is a popular activity, as in many countries, as a means to keep fit. For the less energetic, walking in the large city parks is a favourite pastime, often involving all the family.

Above: Most Mexicans are soccer enthusiasts. The national team, here playing England in 1983, has a devoted following.

Below: Bullfighting was introduced by the Spanish and is still popular, though soccer draws larger crowds.

Left: Mexican cowboys or *charros*, display their riding skill in rodeo-like *charreadas*.

Below: An Indian-style pageant before the church of Our Lady of Guadalupe in Mexico City.

Mexicans take fiestas and festivals very seriously, and celebrate them in style. Their national holidays include Christmas, Independence Day and Labor Day, but many other events, such as those marking Mexico's progress to democracy, are also celebrated. Most towns and villages also have their own local fiestas – usually in honor of their patron saint.

Christmas celebrations are extremely elaborate. On of the highlights for the children is the breaking up of the *piñata*. This is the name given to a brightly painted bag full of toys which is hung from the ceiling. The children are given poles which they use to break open the bag – hoping to bring down the shower of gifts.

At holiday time, many Mexican families like to attend *charreadas*. At these typical Mexican events, horsemen display riding, lassoing and other skills. The *charreadas* derive their name from the traditional costume of the riders, which is similar to that still worn by villagers of the province of Salamanca in Spain at their various fiestas.

News and broadcasting

Mexico has about 390 newspapers, representing all shades of political opinion. The press enjoys great freedom of expression and debates national and international issues in a lively and forthright manner.

Altogether, the newspapers produce a total of nine million copies, putting the country in 13th place in the world in terms of circulation. Mexico City alone has 17 daily papers which print, between them, just under two million copies. Many of the papers have a great number of pages – *Novedades*, for example, may have 90 pages.

Other means of mass communication have also expanded greatly. The country now has, for example, about 1,000 stations broadcasting radio programs, of which about a thousand are commercial. The total number of radios is approximately 25 million, and Mexico has, per person, one of the highest concentrations of radios in the world.

Above: Mexicans are avid newspaper readers and have a free and open press.

Right: A huge range of publications are available, both produced in Mexico and imported. Among the most popular are fashion and sports magazines.

Left: Mexican Television (Televisa) filming an Indian festival in Mexico City.

Below: Jacobo Zabludousky, a popular television presenter.

Bottom: Lucia Mendez, a Mexican television star.

Ownership of television sets is low compared with some countries, as only about 70 per cent of households have sets. Almost a third of these are in Mexico City. The national network, Televisa, has its studios in Mexico City. Throughout the country there are about 200 television stations, of which eight are devoted exclusively to educational and cultural broadcasts. It is also possible to watch programs beamed directly from countries such as the United States.

Book publishing is a very dynamic sector of Mexico's communication industry. The first printing press in the New World was used in Mexico City in 1539, and books have been an important aspect of Mexican culture ever since. Until the 1930s Spanish publishers exported books to Latin America in large numbers. The Spanish Civil War interrupted this trade. Mexico stepped in to fill the gap and it has since then remained a leader in the field. At present, some 5,000 titles are published in Mexico each year. Most are in Spanish and go to markets on both sides of the Atlantic.

Fact file: home life and leisure

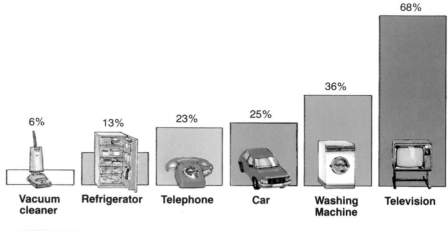

68%

36%

25%

23%

13%

6%

| Vacuum cleaner | Refrigerator | Telephone | Car | Washing Machine | Television |

Other goods and services	5%
Clothing and shoes	8%
Vehicles	11%
Education and Amusement	15%
Housing	17%
Food	44%

△ **How many households owned goods in the 1980s**

The ownership of television sets and other consumer durables, are low in comparison with the US and European countries. There has been a surge in ownership of such goods in recent years.

◁ **How the average household budget is spent**
Rents in Mexico are quite low. Education and entertainment are an increasing part of family expenditure.

▽ **Mexican stamps and money**
The *peso* is divided into 100 *centavos*. Banknotes come in denominations of 100, 500, 1,000, 2,000, 5,000 and 10,000 *pesos*. There are coins of 1, 5, 10 and 50 *pesos* and also coins of 20 and 50 *centavos*.

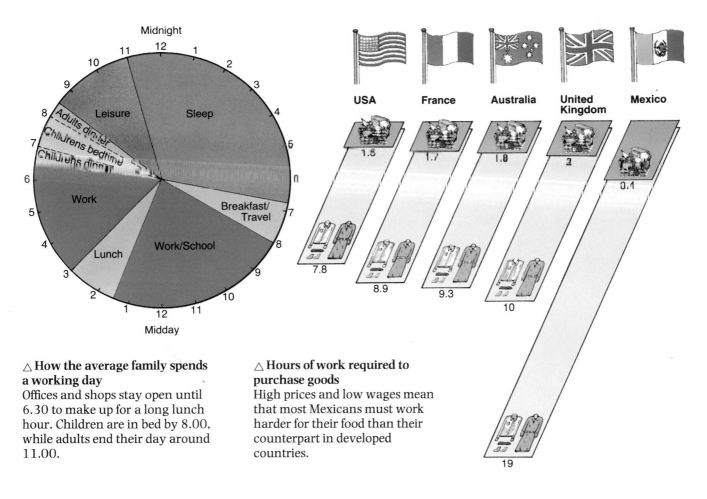

△ How the average family spends a working day
Offices and shops stay open until 6.30 to make up for a long lunch hour. Children are in bed by 8.00, while adults end their day around 11.00.

△ Hours of work required to purchase goods
High prices and low wages mean that most Mexicans must work harder for their food than their counterpart in developed countries.

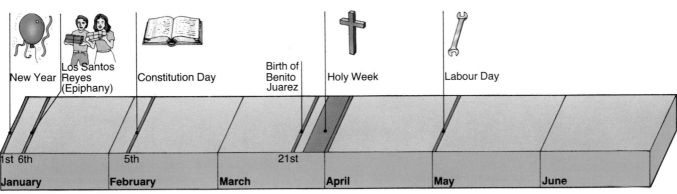

The main holidays and festivals in Mexico
Many official holidays commemorate historical events. Religious feasts are observed as well.

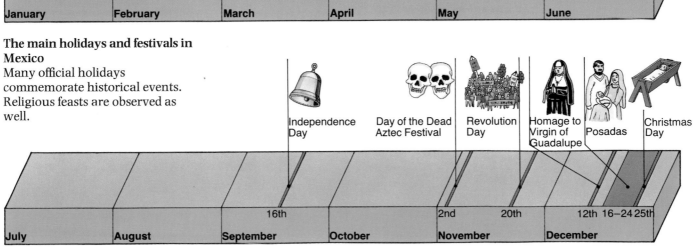

Farming and fishing

Only about half of Mexico is suitable for agriculture because of Mexico's dry climate and rugged mountainous terrain. In some parts of the country artificial irrigation is needed throughout the year.

Until the 19th century, most of Mexico was in the hands of a few powerful landowners. Since then there have been laws and reforms to redistribute the land, some of it is farmed under the *ejido* system. Under this system the government owns the land, but allocates certain areas to people who work it and then keep the profits. Farmers grow both food crops (which are used to feed themselves), and cash crops which are sold in the markets and also exported.

The main commercial farming areas are in irrigated parts of the north of the country, where cotton and wheat are the chief crops. Fruit and vegetables, such as melons and tomatoes, are grown along the fertile river valleys.

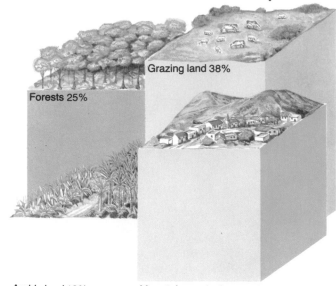

Forests 25%

Grazing land 38%

Arable land 12%

Mountains and urban 25%

Above: Land use in Mexico. The scarce arable land, where necessary, is irrigated to make it yield more crops.

Below: Ox-drawn carts, unchanged for centuries, are still a common sight in many rural areas of Mexico.

Above: Mexico grows a large amount of fruit. Apples, bananas and citrus fruits grow well along the river valleys.

Right: The blue agave plant is the source of the strong drink called *tequila*.

Below: Fishing nets on the Pacific Coast.

Mexico is the world's sixth largest meat producer. Cattle are reared in semi-arid areas of the north, and sheep are grazed on the Central Plateau. The most rugged areas are suitable only for goats.

Sugar cane, coffee, and fruit are important crops on the southern plains. Fruit production has expanded greatly in recent years. But grains are the main crops, especially corn, the chief food crop, which is grown on nearly half the cultivated lands. Even so, Mexico still has to import corn to satisfy demand.

With the introduction of refrigerated trucks, fishing has developed into a major industry. It provides employment not only for fishermen, but also for retailers and distributors who handle the catches of tuna, sardines, anchovies, squid and a variety of shellfish. The most important catches are of shrimp, many thousand tons of which are exported.

Forestry is becoming increasingly important. Most of the timber, which includes both hard and soft woods, is used for lumber.

Natural resources

Mexico's greatest asset has always been its mineral wealth. The Spanish swiftly developed the rich silver deposits of Mexico. In recent times the discovery and exploitation of oil and gas has helped the growth of Mexican industry.

Mexico was already one of the world's major oil producers in 1922, but it was the huge new reserves discovered along the gulf coast and offshore in 1976 that provided the revenues for the beginning of an industrial boom. By 1988 the country was producing 143 million tons of oil a year, nearly one-twentieth of world production. Mexico is now the world's fourth largest oil producer, and the fifth largest in the production of natural gas.

The many rivers which cascade down the steep valleys of the Central Plateau provide Mexico with vast amounts of hydroelectric power. Today over one-third of Mexico's energy requirements are provided by hydroelectric schemes.

Below: A large hydro-electric dam at Villahermosa. More than a third of Mexico's electricity is generated by hydro-electric plants.

Above: Oil production in Mexico is government controlled by PEMEX (Petroleos Mexicanos). Its revenues are vital to Mexico's economy.

Mexico is also endowed with a great many precious metals and other minerals that are vital to industry. The country leads the world in silver production, is second in the production of graphite and bismuth, third in mercury production, and fourth in arsenic and selenium.

Other important minerals include sulphur, lead, zinc, coal, uranium, iron ore, gold and copper. Minerals represent the fourth largest source of export revenue for Mexico after oil, agricultural products and machinery.

Mining employs over 160,000 people directly, with another 1.6 million people involved in related industries.

Some of the minerals, such as coal, provide primary sources of energy while others are used to make vital components in manufacturing. The country's large cement industry gets its raw materials, sand, gravel and crushed stone, from local quarries. Mexico's large craft industry draws on the nation's vast deposits of precious metals, especially silver.

Above left: Mexico's main steel works are located at Monterrey and Monclova, close to the Sabinas coalfields.

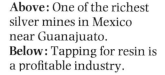

Above: One of the richest silver mines in Mexico near Guanajuato.
Below: Tapping for resin is a profitable industry.

Industry and trade

Mexico's economy flourished during the oil boom of the 1970s, creating many new jobs. A fall in world oil prices in the 1980s slowed the expansion considerably, but much of the nation's industry is now sufficiently modernized to compete in world markets.

Most of Mexico's industry is located around Mexico City, Guadalajara, Orizaba and Puebla. Farther north, extensive coalfields fuel the iron and steel plants at the nearby cities of Monterrey and Monclova.

Oil, gas and products from the petrochemical industry are the chief sources of overseas currency, and represent more than 60 per cent of all exports. Mexico's main trading partners are the United States and Japan, Europe and Latin America.

Increased car ownership has been one of the most visible signs of the country's economic progress. Today, demand for cars exceeds production. Until the 1960s, car factories merely assembled parts made elsewhere. But today Mexico also makes vehicle parts.

Above: Car manufacture and assembly is an increasingly important industry. Here, a Chevrolet is ready to leave the assembly line.

Left: Food processing accounts for one quarter of Mexico's industrial production, and employs half a million people. This plant is producing *tequila*.

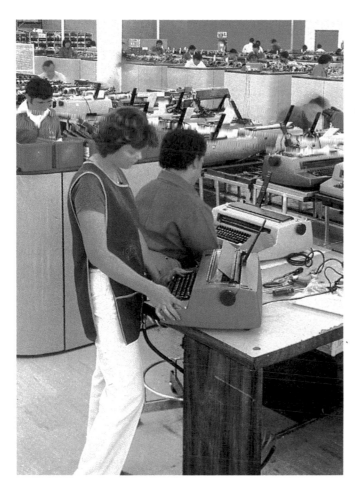

Tourism is the second largest source of currency in Mexico. The country's rich and colorful heritage, as well as its breathtaking scenery and extensive beaches, attracted 5,407,000 visitors in 1987. One of the most famous resorts is Acapulco on the western Pacific coast, although the Caribbean coast boasts equally fine beaches with the added attractions of the Yucatán Peninsula and its Mayan ruins.

Food processing, electronics and the production of office equipment, are all part of Mexico's light industry, These and other activities are closely related to the tourist industry, They include glassware, textiles, woollen goods and handicrafts. Products based on traditional designs range from gold and silver jewelry to basketware.

Other important industries in Mexico include the construction industry, which employs seven per cent of the working population, and the manufacture of timber products.

Above left: Typewriters being assembled at a large IBM factory in Mexico City.

Above: A tourist resort.
Below: Traditional designs are popular with tourists.

Transportation

Mexico has a modern and extensive system of highways despite the mountainous nature of the country. There are more than 100,000 km (62,140 miles) of proper paved macadam roads, many of which converge on Mexico City and provincial capitals, such as Guadalajara. Routes radiating from Mexico City connect the capital with other major towns and ports. Running the length of the country is the Pan American Highway, a highway system linking the United States with 17 Latin American countries.

In 1985 the total number of motor vehicles in Mexico exceeded seven million, of which 70.5 per cent were cars and 29.5 per cent were trucks or buses. About two-fifths of the nation's motor vehicles are found in Mexico City.

In the cities buses are inexpensive and run frequently. Buses are a popular means of transport and come in all shapes and sizes from luxury coaches with air conditioning which are used for long journeys and old, rattling vehicles which serve the isolated rural districts.

Above: This ferry or *panga* crosses the Grijalva River in the southern state of Tabasco. It provides an essential link for many people.

Below: A shared taxi and a bus on a highway out of Mexico City. Both are popular and inexpensive forms of transport in Mexico.

Above: An airliner from Aero-mexico's fleet at Villahermosa, in the southern part of the Gulf of Mexico.

Right: Mexico has 26,300 km (16,300 miles) of railway which has to traverse very often difficult terrain.

Air transport has expanded greatly in recent years. By the 1980s some 20 million passengers passed through Mexico's airports during the course of a year.

The main shipping ports are at Veracruz, Tampico, Coatzalcoacos, Salina Cruz, Manzanillo, Acapulco and Lázaro Cardenas. Veracruz, on the Gulf of Mexico, is the leading port. Located close by are the installations of Pajaritos, which handle most of the shipments for the petroleum industry.

The railroads are government-run apart from three small lines in private hands. The state railroads receive a subsidy which makes the fares cheap and the cargo rates especially low. For this reason more cargo is moved by rail in Mexico than in many other more industrialized countries. Mexico City also has a subway system, decorated in Indian, Mexican and Spanish styles. It is as crowded during rush hours as any similar system elsewhere.

Fact file: economy and trade

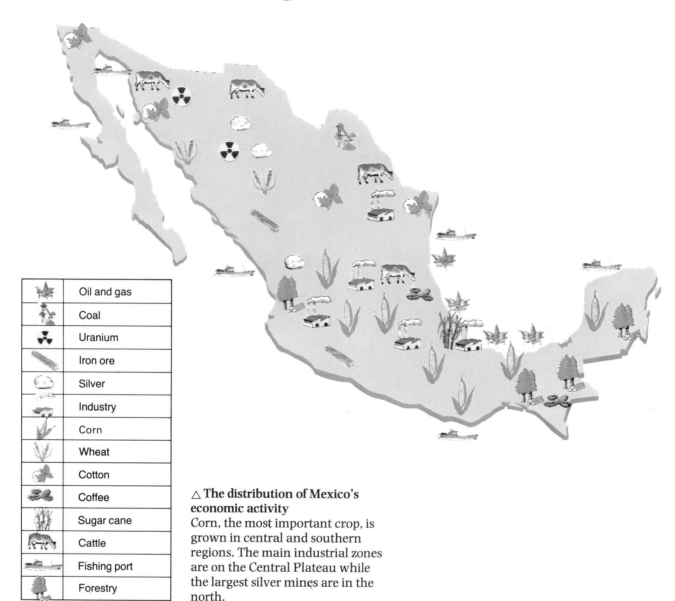

	Oil and gas
	Coal
	Uranium
	Iron ore
	Silver
	Industry
	Corn
	Wheat
	Cotton
	Coffee
	Sugar cane
	Cattle
	Fishing port
	Forestry

△ **The distribution of Mexico's economic activity**
Corn, the most important crop, is grown in central and southern regions. The main industrial zones are on the Central Plateau while the largest silver mines are in the north.

Key facts

Structure of production: Of the total GDP (the value of all economic activity in Mexico), farming, forestry and fishing contribute 9 per cent, industry 34 per cent, and services (such as commerce and the civil service) 57 per cent.
Farming: Crops are grown on about 12 per cent of Mexico's land area. Grazing land makes up another 38 per cent. *Main products:* cotton, coffee, fruit, wheat, sorghum, corn.

sugar cane, vegetables.
Mining: In the early 1980s, Mexico became the second largest oil producer in the Americas, overtaking Venezuela. Other minerals include silver, coal, iron, copper, gold, lead, sulphur, manganese, tin, uranium and zinc.
Manufacturing: Mexico has expanded its manufacturing industries greatly in the last 40 years. Major products now include chemicals, machinery, clothing, processed foods, processed

petroleum and steel.
Trade (1985): Total imports: US $13,994 million; exports: US $21,820 million. Mexico is the fourth most important trading Nation in the Americas, after the US, Canada and Brazil.
Economic growth: The average growth rate of Mexico's gross national product between 1980 and 1988 was 0.7 per cent a year. This slow rate reflected a major recession in the economy, caused by a fall in world oil prices.

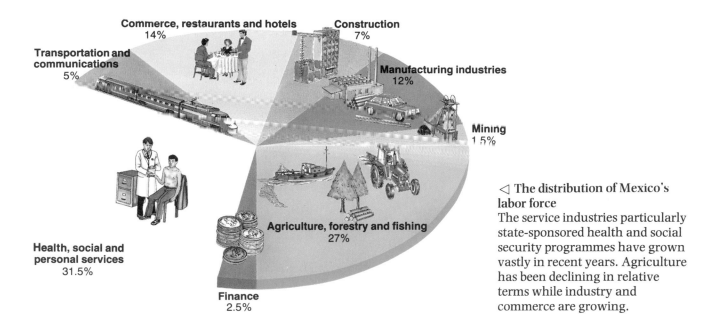

Transportation and communications 5%

Commerce, restaurants and hotels 14%

Construction 7%

Manufacturing industries 12%

Mining 1.5%

Agriculture, forestry and fishing 27%

Health, social and personal services 31.5%

Finance 2.5%

◁ The distribution of Mexico's labor force
The service industries particularly state-sponsored health and social security programmes have grown vastly in recent years. Agriculture has been declining in relative terms while industry and commerce are growing.

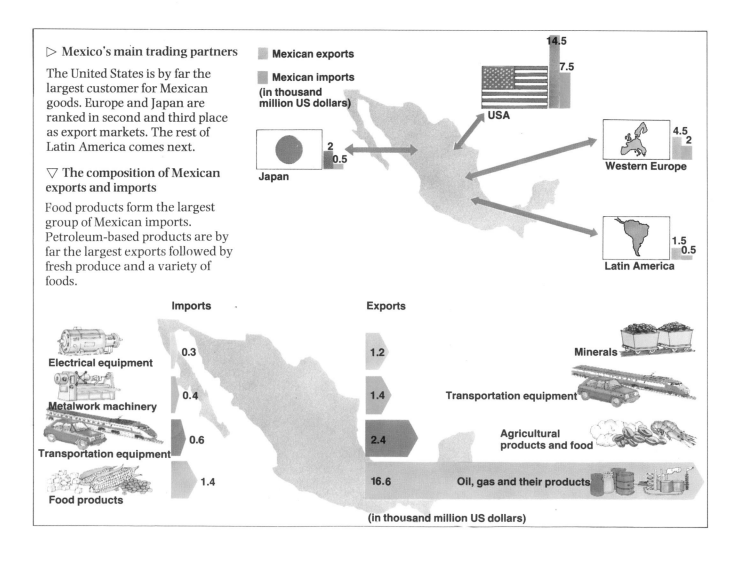

▷ Mexico's main trading partners

The United States is by far the largest customer for Mexican goods. Europe and Japan are ranked in second and third place as export markets. The rest of Latin America comes next.

▽ The composition of Mexican exports and imports

Food products form the largest group of Mexican imports. Petroleum-based products are by far the largest exports followed by fresh produce and a variety of foods.

Mexican exports

Mexican imports (in thousand million US dollars)

USA 14.5 / 7.5

Japan 2 / 0.5

Western Europe 4.5 / 2

Latin America 1.5 / 0.5

Imports

Electrical equipment 0.3
Metalwork machinery 0.4
Transportation equipment 0.6
Food products 1.4

Exports

Minerals 1.2
Transportation equipment 1.4
Agricultural products and food 2.4
Oil, gas and their products 16.6

(in thousand million US dollars)

Education

Few developing countries have expanded education as vigorously as Mexico. After the 1910 Revolution, hundreds of schools were opened throughout the country. The fight for literacy gradually brought results, with a great leap forward between 1960 and 1980. By 1988. The number of people who could read and write has risen to 95 per cent.

In Mexico education is compulsory and free between the ages of six and 16. Before the age of six, some Mexican children attend a pre-school course for two years. Primary (elementary) education lasts six years and is divided into two levels, basic and higher, each taking three years. Secondary education consists of a three-year basic curriculum, and a further three years for pupils intending to go to university.

Primary school children begin their day at 8 in the morning and finish at 1.00 p.m. Modern teaching methods are used in Mexican schools, but discipline is strict and the teacher still a figure of respect.

Above: A primary school. Education at Mexican primary schools is free and compulsory from the age of six.

Left: The government has allocated large sums of money to build new schools and supply educational equipment for the growing population of Mexicans.

Left: Pupils using the school's computers. Many classrooms have this type of modern equipment.

Below: Students at the National University of Mexico City. A vast mosaic decorates the main library building.

Since education in Mexico is now compulsory, nearly all children are registered at a school. Mexico has achieved enrollment figures of 98 per cent for children of primary school age, and 88 per cent for children of secondary level. Even remote areas can now receive educational broadcasts by means of Mexico's recently launched communications satellite.

Most schools in Mexico are government run. There are also many church schools which are not supported by the government. They make, however, a very valuable contribution to the educational system, especially at the secondary-school level.

For the student who goes on to higher education there are more than 300 professional schools, including state universities, teacher-training schools and technical colleges. In 1988 over a million students were pursuing higher education. The country's oldest and largest university is in Mexico City.

The arts

The many great Indian civilizations have provided Mexico with a vast cultural treasures, including beautiful temples and impressive sculptures. Folk arts derived from ancient Indian cultures still survive. The ceramic, weaving and silverwork crafts are particularly distinguished.

But art is by no means a thing of the past in Mexico. In the early 20th century, a number of Mexican artists achieved lasting fame for their new approach to mural painting. These included José Clemente Orozco (1883–1949), David Siqueiros (1898–1974), Diego Rivera (1886–1957), and Rufino Tamayo (1899–).

Among the country's most noted composers is Carlos Chávez (1899–1978,) whose symphonic and chamber music has become part of the modern repertoire in both America and Europe. In 1952 the Mexican dancer Amalia Hernández formed the Ballet Folklórico. This dance group has two companies touring the world, and a third at the Palace of Fine Arts in Mexico City.

Above: A Mayan sculpture. Mexico's Indian heritage is the inspiration of many of its 20th century artists.

Below: *The Time Machine* is one of Diego Rivera's colourful murals which depict social and political themes in world history.

Left: Sor Juana Inés de la Cruz, the brilliant and outspoken writer. Her prose and poetry rank among the finest of the 17th century.

Above: Octavio Paz, poet, critic and interpreter of the Mexican character.

Below: The entrance to Mexico City's Satellite Town.

But it is in literature that Mexico has, perhaps, made the greatest contribution to world culture. A long line of poets, dramatists, political writers and novelists have enriched the literature of both Spain and the New World. Among them is a 17th-century nun Sor (Sister) Juana Inés de la Cruz (1651–95), whose poetry ranks with the finest in the Spanish language. Her interest in politics and her scientific mind made her a remarkable person, far ahead of her time.

Mexico has also produced such modern writers as Juan Rulfo (1918–86), Carlos Fuentes (1928–) and Octavio Paz (1914–). Rulfo was the founder of the "magical realism" school of fiction, while Fuentes remains at the forefront of Latin American novelists. The leading writer in contemporary Mexico is the poet and essayist Octavio Paz, whose works, like those of Fuentes, have been translated into most Western languages. His writings shed great light on the Mexican personality.

The making of modern Mexico

Mexico gained independence from Spain in 1821. The new government, however, could do little to improve conditions for the common people, because the rich, landed classes still effectively ruled the country.

In 1836, north of the Rio Grande, settlers from the United States revolted against Mexican rule, and proclaimed the Republic of Texas. General López de Santa Anna rode north to the settlers' fort – an old mission called "The Poplar" (El Alamo) – and killed most of the defenders. One month later the United States army attacked and defeated the Mexican army.

In 1846 American forces stormed Mexico City. Peace came when Santa Anna, then president, ceded Texas – and later California, New Mexico and parts of Arizona – to the United States. Benito Juárez, Minister of Justice, then ordered all church and army property seized and given to the needy. Conservative groups fought these measures and a bitter civil war ensued.

Above: General López de Santa Anna, President of Mexico during the war with the United States in 1846–7.

Left: The Alamo

Below: The land acquired by the United States from Mexico during and after the Mexican War. Mexico lost half of its land area.

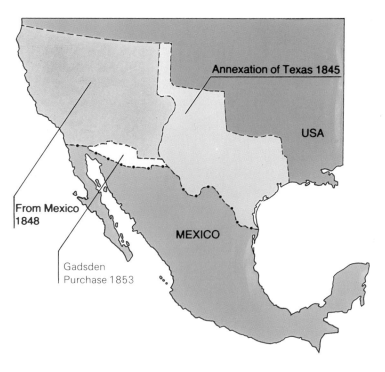

Annexation of Texas 1845

USA

From Mexico 1848

Gadsden Purchase 1853

MEXICO

Above: Archduke Maximilian of Austria is executed by firing squad in 1867. He was emperor of Mexico for only three years.

Right: Porfirio Díaz was President of Mexico for more than 30 years.
Below right: Peasants in revolt against the Díaz regime in 1910.

The war brought ruin to the economy and Juárez decided to delay payment of money owed to Spain, Britain and France. Soon all three countries landed troops to press their claims, but only the French chose to fight. Defeated initially at the Battle of Puebla (1862), France eventually routed Juárez.

In 1864 Mexican exiles, restored to power by the French, installed Archduke Maximilian of Austria as emperor. It was a short reign. Maximilian was captured in battle by Juárist forces in 1867, and promptly shot.

Under Porfirio Díaz's presidency (1876–1910), foreign investment grew. A thriving middle class also emerged, though peasants and workers still lacked the most basic human rights.

The sufferings of the poor exploded in the Mexican Revolution of 1910. It continued until the early 1930s, when socialist values became national policy. The Revolutionary Party, founded in 1929, assumed power that year and has remained in office ever since.

Mexico in the modern world

The oil boom begun in the 1970s brought enormous benefits to Mexico. It also posed a great problem – how to pay back the vast sums of money borrowed from other countries to develop a modern oil industry.

Despite the enormous strides made by Mexico, it became clear that the income produced by petroleum was not sufficient to meet repayments of the debt. Worse still, a drop in the price of oil in the 1980s meant the country's revenues were reduced.

In the late 1980s the Mexican government sought to obtain new terms for repayments of the debt. It also fought an economic recession, accompanied by soaring unemployment and an annual inflation rate of 69 per cent. How well it copes with these problems will determine Mexico's future. If the government succeeds in reducing inflation and maintaining economic growth, there will be no loss of the benefits brought by the boom, and some hope of renewed growth in the future.

Above: The old and new in Mexico City. Sub-standard houses contrast sharply with modern high-rise buildings.

Left: Soccer fans at a match, during the World Cup, held in Mexico in 1986. Mexico has hosted several major events in recent years, including the Olympic Games.

Left: Rodolfo Neri, the first Mexican astronaut, went on a Space Shuttle mission in 1985. He was a crew member on a flight of the *Atlantis* shuttle.

Above: Carlos Salinas de Gortari became President of Mexico in 1988.
Below: Mexico has a vast young population.

Relations between Mexico and the United States have become strained over the problem of migration. For decades, Mexicans have crossed the Rio Grande by the thousands in search of work. Lacking papers, few find new jobs, while virtually all are subject to arrest and even detention for illegally entering the United States.

To the south, Mexico is witnessing the unrest in El Salvador, Honduras, Guatemala and Nicaragua. As the leading voice of the Contadora Group – a regional alliance that includes Venezuela, Panama and Colombia – the Mexican government is pressing for a diplomatic solution to the crisis in Central America, a dangerous powder keg on its doorstep.

Its role in this and other regional problems is a significant one. Mexico is seen by other Latin American countries as an experienced negotiator with the United States, and is a leading spokesman for the nations that share its Spanish and Latin American traditions.

Fact file: government and world role

Key facts

Official name: *Estados Unidos Mexicanos* (United Mexican States)

National flag: Three vertical stripes of green, white and red. The central white stripe bears the coat of arms, which depicts an eagle on a cactus holding a snake.

National anthem: *Mexicanos, al grito de guerra.* (Mexicans, when you hear the war cry.)

National government: Mexico is a democratic federal republic. *Head of State:* The president, who is directly elected to a single, six-year term. The president heads the government and appoints the council of ministers and senior military and civilian officers of the state.

Congress: The General Congress, the law-making parliament, consists of a 64-member Senate and a 500 member Chamber of Deputies. Senators serve six-year terms and deputies three-year terms.

Local government: The 31 states each have an elected governor and a Chamber of Deputies. The Federal District (Mexico City) is administered by a governor appointed by the president. The states are divided into local government areas, each with elected presidents and councils.

Defence: Enlistment into the regular army is voluntary, but for men aged 18 there is conscription into a part-time militia. *Army:* In 1989, the Army had a strength of 105,500. *Air Force:* The strength of the Air Force was about 7,000. *Navy:* In 1989, the Navy had 30,000 personnel.

Economic alliances: Mexico is a member of the Latin American Integration Association (LAIA), which took over from the Latin American Free Trade Association (LAFTA) in 1981.

Political alliances: Mexico is a member of the United Nations and of the OAS (Organization of American States), which is a regional organization of the United Nations. It is also a leading member of the Contadora Group (Mexico, Venezuela, Panama and Colombia).

Members of Organization of American States (OAS)

Members of Latin American Integration Association (LAIA)

△ **Mexico in the Americas** Mexico forms part of the Organization of American States which has its headquarters in Washington. It is also a member of the United Nations. The Latin American Integration Association (LAIA), fosters trade among the states south of the Rio Grande.

The Mexican system of government

The legislative, executive and judicial branches of the government are kept separate.

The Chamber of Deputies has 500 members while the Senate has 64 – two from each state and two from the Federal District. The president has supreme executive powers and appoints the Council of Ministers. He is elected for a single six-year term by direct suffrage.

President

GOVERNMENT

Council of Ministers (Cabinet)

CONGRESS OF THE UNION (PARLIAMENT)

Chamber of Duputies

Senate

Electorate

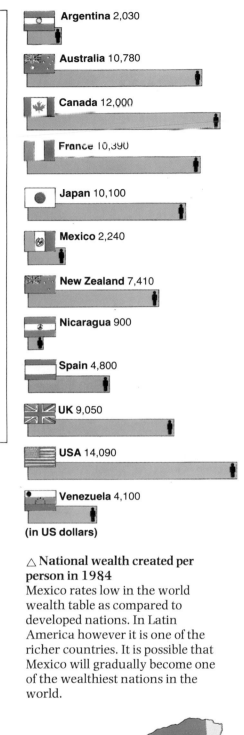

Argentina 2,030

Australia 10,780

Canada 12,000

France 10,390

Japan 10,100

Mexico 2,240

New Zealand 7,410

Nicaragua 900

Spain 4,800

UK 9,050

USA 14,090

Venezuela 4,100

(in US dollars)

△ **National wealth created per person in 1984**

Mexico rates low in the world wealth table as compared to developed nations. In Latin America however it is one of the richer countries. It is possible that Mexico will gradually become one of the wealthiest nations in the world.

1 Federal District
2 México
3 Tlaxcala
4 Puebla
5 Morelos
6 Hidalgo
7 Querétaro
8 Guanajuato
9 Aguascalientes

△ **The States of Mexico**

Baja California Norte
Baja California Sur
Sonora
Chihuahua
Coahuila
Sinaloa
Nuevo León
Durango
Zacatecas
Tamaulipas
San Luis Potosí
Nayarit
Jalisco
Michoacán
Colima
Guerrero
VeraCruz
Oaxaca
Chiapas
Tabasco
Campeche
Yucatán
Quintana Roo

Index

Acapulco 7, 11, 14, 33, 35
Agriculture 28, 37
Air transportation 13, 35, 36
Altitude 7
Ancient traditions 5
Architecture 11
Arts 40
Azteca Stadium 22
Aztecs, the 8, 12

Baja California 6, 10, 14, 15
Ballet Folklórico 40
Battle of Puebla 43
Broadcasting 24
Bullfighting 22

Car manufacture 32
Cattle 29, 36
Central Plateau 7, 10, 15, 29, 30
Charreadas 23
Chavez, Carlos 40
Chili Con Carne 21
Cities 10, 11, 14, 15
Civil War 25, 42
Climate 6, 7, 28
Clothing manufacture 13
Communications 10, 24, 39
Contadora Group 45, 46
Cooking 17, 20
Corn 21, 29, 36
Craft industry 31
Crops 28, 29, 36
Culture 13, 41
Customs 5

Defense 46
Deserts 6
Díaz, Porfirio 43
Drinks 20, 29

Economic growth 32, 36, 44
Economy 13, 43
Education 13, 16, 38, 39
Electricity 13
Energy 30, 31, 36
Europe 32
Exports 28, 29, 32, 36, 37

Families 16, 17, 26, 27
Farming 28, 36
Fiestas 23, 27
Fishing 28, 29, 36
Food 7, 18, 20, 21
Food processing 13, 32, 33
Forestry 29, 31, 36
Fuentes, Carlos 41

Gas 30
Goats 29, 36
Government 12, 28, 42, 44, 46, 47
Guadalajara 10, 14, 19, 32
Gulf of Mexico 6, 35

Health Services 9
Hernández, Amalia 40
Highways 34
Home life 16
Household budget 26
Households 16, 26
Hydroelectric power 30, 36

Imports 29, 36, 37
Independence 42
Indian culture 5
Indians 8
Industry 5, 13, 29, 30, 32, 33, 37
Irrigation 42

Japan 32
Juárez, Benito 42, 43

Lake Chapala 14
Land area 14
Land use 28
Language 14
Latin America 5, 32, 34
Latin American Integration Association (LAIA) 46
Latin American Tower 12
Life Expectancy 26
Life Styles 5, 11
Lowlands 6

Manufacturing 31, 36
Markets 18, 28
Maximilian, Archduke 43
Maya 8, 14
Mayan ruins 33
Meals 20
Meat production 29
Mestizos 8
Mexico City 10, 11, 12, 13, 14, 19, 32
Migration 10, 45
Minerals 30, 31, 36
Mining 31, 36
Mixtec 8, 14
Monclava 32
Money 26
Monterrey 10, 14, 32
Motor vehicles 34
Mountains 7, 13, 28
Municipal services 11
Museum of Anthropology 13

National anthem 46
National Palace 12
Natural resouces 30
News 24
Newspapers 24
Neri, Rodolfo 45

Oil 13, 30, 32, 44
Olympic games 22
Organization of American States (OAS) 46
Orizaba (Citalatépetl) 7, 14, 32
Orozco, José Clemente 40
Overseas currency 32

Palace of Fine Arts 13, 40
Pan American Highway 34
Paseo de la Reforma 12
Pastimes 22
Paz, Octavio 41
Peninsulas 6, 10, 14
People 5, 8
Petroleos Mexicanos (PEMEX) 30
Pollution 11, 13
Popacatépetl 7
Population 8, 9, 10, 13, 14, 15, 26
Ports 11, 34, 35
Precious metals 31
President, The 45, 46, 47
Prices 26
Publishing 24, 25
Puebla 14, 32

Radios 17, 24
Rail transportation 13, 35, 36
Religion 26
Restaurants 21
Revolution of 1910 9, 38, 43
Rio Grande 14, 15
Rivera, Diego 40
Rivers 14, 30
Road transport 13, 34, 36
Rulfo, Juan 41

Santa Anna, General López de 42
Sheep 29, 36
Shipping 36
Shops 18, 19
Sierra Madre Occidental 6, 7
Sierra Madre Oriental 7
Silver 30, 31
Siqueiros, David 40
Soccer 22
Sor Juana Inés de la Cruz 41
Southern highlands 7
Spaniards 8, 12, 30
Spanish culture 5
Sport 22
Stamps 26
Subway system 12

Tacos 21
Tamayo, Rufino 40
Technology 5
Television 17, 25, 26
Temperature 6
Tenochtitlán 12

Textiles 13, 33
Toltec 8
Tortillas 21
Tourism 13, 19, 33
Towns 10, 11, 15
Trade 26, 32
Trading partners 32, 37
Tribes 8
Tropical forests 6

United Nations (UN) 46
United States 5, 32, 34, 37, 42
University 13, 39

Vacations 26, 27
Vegetation 6, 7
Veracruz 35
Villages 10, 18
Volcanoes 7, 14

Workforce 13, 26, 37
Working hours 26, 27
World Cup 22, 45

Yucatán Peninsula 6, 10, 14, 15, 33

Zapotec 8, 14
Zócalo 12